MW01132468

For my quintessential British friend
and editor, Laura, who taught me
what a quince was.

The Queen has a Question.

Does a
Quick Quail
say
"QUACK"?

Does a Quarter of a Quiche say "QUACK"?

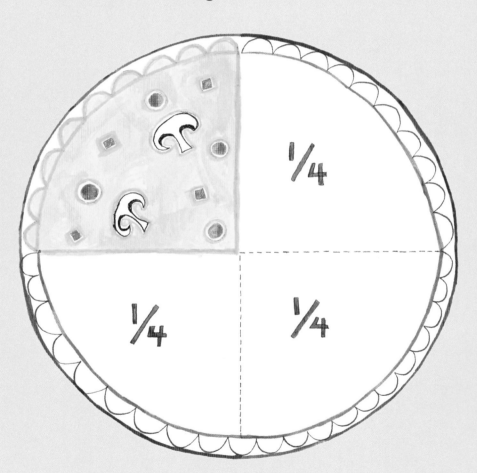

Does a Quince on a
Quilt say "QUACK"?

Does a Quoll in a Queue say "QUACK"?

QUEUE
STARTS
HERE →

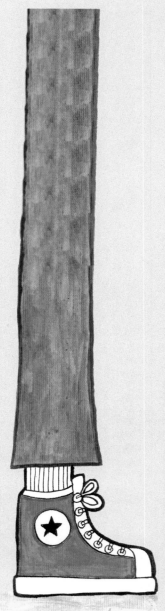

Does a Quart of Quarters say "QUACK"?

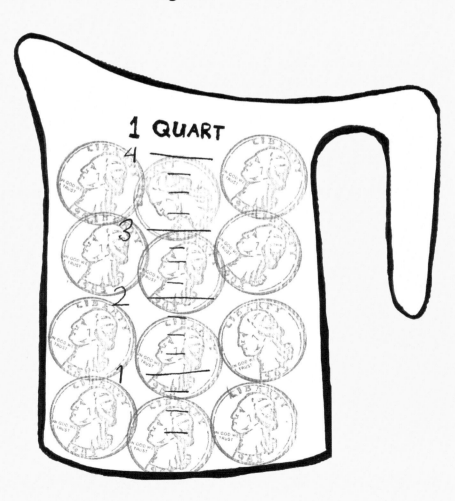

Does a Quiet Quiz say "QUACK"?

Does a duck eating Quinoa say "QUACK"?

YES!
A duck says
"QUACK"!!

words in
this book:

QUEEN

QUAIL

QUEUE

An area where a line of people wait.

QUEUE STARTS HERE →

QUOLL

A carnivorous (meat-eating) marsupial that lives in Australia, New Guinea and Tasmania. It mostly comes out at night.

QUICHE

A savory pie filled with eggs, cheese, meat and vegetables.

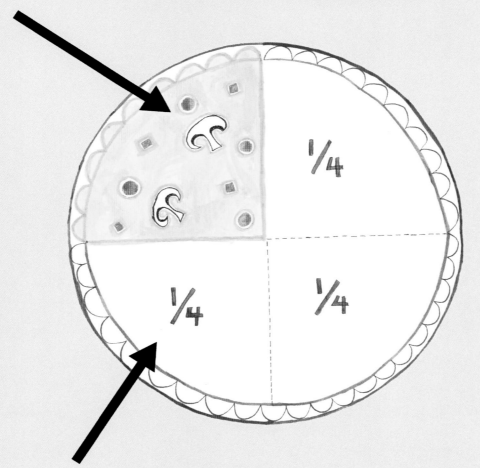

QUARTER

1 of 4 equal parts of something.

QUINCE

A fruit that is similar to a pear or apple, but is very sour when eaten uncooked.

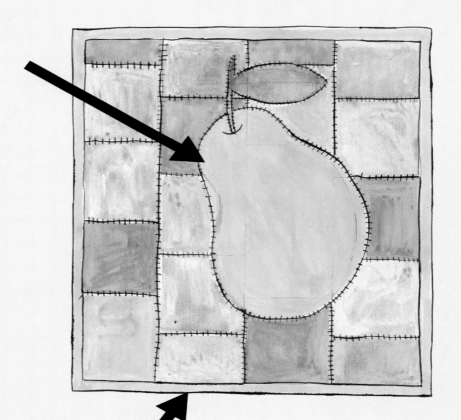

QUILT

A blanket made by sewing together 3 layers of fabric, with a colorful design on top.

QUIZ

A short test used at school.

QUINOA

A grain originaly from South America,
that can be cooked and eaten like rice.

QUART

A quart is a unit of volume, equal to a quarter of a gallon.

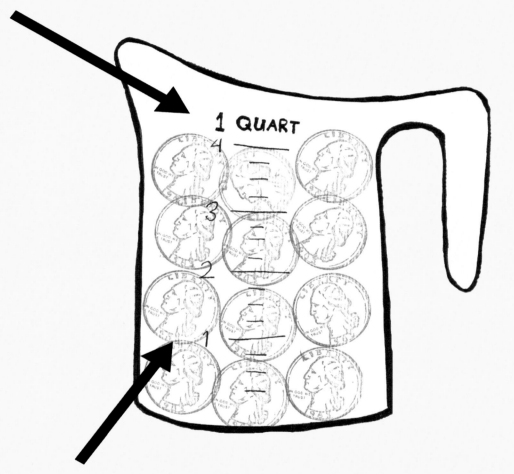

1 QUART

QUARTERS

Quarters are United States coins, valued at one-fourth of a U.S. dollar.

Q is for QUILL Pen

Use a QUILL pen and ink to draw a picture.

Q is for QUILL Pen

The queen has a question.

AlphaBOX Book Series

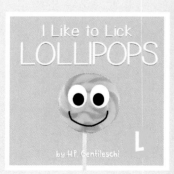

MILK in My Mailbox
by H.P. Gentileschi
M

Does a NUT have a NOSE?
by H.P. Gentileschi
N

ONE OCTOPUS in the Olive Tree
by H.P. Gentileschi
O

penguin's paper plane
by H.P. Gentileschi
P

The Queen's Question
by H.P. Gentileschi
Q

Rabbit's Rainbow in Rome
by H.P. Gentileschi
R

Snake's Snacks
by H.P. Gentileschi
S

Does a Tomato Have Teeth?
by H.P. Gentileschi
T

Under My Umbrella
by H.P. Gentileschi
U

Victoria's Violin
by H.P. Gentileschi
V

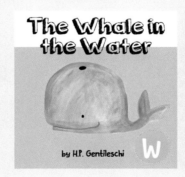

The Whale in the Water
by H.P. Gentileschi
W

Fox Has A Box
by H.P. Gentileschi
X

YOUR YELLOW YO-YO
by H.P. Gentileschi
Y

Zero Zebras in the ZOO!
by H.P. Gentileschi
Z

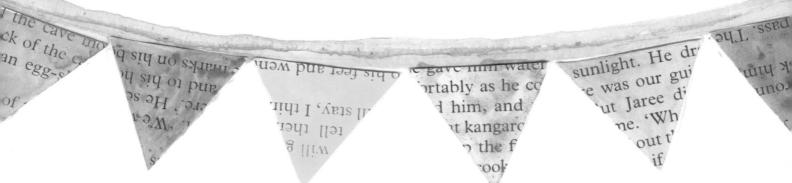

For more engaging activities, teaching resources and to learn more about AlphaBOX books, follow H.P. Gentileschi on:

H.P. Gentileschi

www.hpgentileschi.com
hpgentileschi@gmail.com

We'd love to see how you're using the AlphaBOX series!
Share and tag your photos using:
#alphaboxbooks

Made in the USA
Middletown, DE
13 January 2023

22127137R00015